The Heartache That Birthed You

Amairani Llerena

Presentation by *BookLeaf Publishing*

Web: www.bookleafpub.com

E-mail: info@bookleafpub.com

ISBN: 9789357744201

First edition 2022

To all those that have made an impact on my life—

be it good or bad; thank you.

To my fabulous 5, my cornerstone, mi familia:

gracias por todo el amor y el apoyo.

To my Tako: you are my legacy, the light of my life,

my first true love.

You've given me a greater purpose.

This book was born out of a necessity to write. After many therapy sessions, some intense soul-searching and self-mandatory reflections, I decided I could no longer keep these words hidden in the folders of my mind. Having struggled with depression and anxiety most of my adult life, one of my therapists feared postpartum depression would hit me deeply. And truthfully, it did. It made me realize that certain things, if not all, fade away. Nothing is concrete. Relationships, dreams, goals, successes and losses; all of them are just seasons. This season of my life is one I chose to expose, in hopes that others struggling through similar situations can find a form of relief through the vulnerability of my words.

Healing is not linear, and mine has been a slow progression that can often feel like a digression if left alone for too long. This book is a solace, an escape into the dark corners of my mind where I felt most necessary to inspect.

I would like to begin by expressing my gratitude to those who encouraged me to push for the publication of this book: Gibel Amador and Isabel Mayagoitia, without whom I would not have found the courage to do so. I'd also like to thank Isaac Betances for his collaboration on the cover artwork; it is an absolute honor to feature your beautiful art. To Sonia and the amazing team at Bookleaf Publishing, thank you for making my dream a reality. Arid, my brother and soulmate, thank you for being an active part of my child's life, from birthing classes, birth day, and caring for him thereafter. You are one of my greatest supporters and I'd be lost without you. To Manny Jay Loya, whose photography can be found on the back cover. Thank you for your friendship and for capturing many beautiful moments with my Kahlo. To Mauricio Ibave, thank you for your creative contribution towards the completion of this book. Every input and suggestion you gave was taken with an open heart and I am eternally grateful for the time you took to look over my work. Lastly, I want to thank Richie Marrufo, for always pushing me to continue writing poetry and for always providing a safe space for local talent to express their intimate thoughts. The Barbed Wire Open Mic Series has saved my life.

A Toast to Past Lovers

Embodiment of passion;
Epitome of enlightenment.
Every word he spoke
sparked in my being
a curiosity for life and its wonders;
Never had I encountered
such a profound soul.
His gaze was entrapment,
His touch, an addiction.
He could make you feel moons and
light years away
yet ever present
in the wrinkle of that time.
Through his existence in my life,
I learned to explore the
wondrous corners of imagination,
I accepted disbeliefs that
I would have otherwise rejected.
He was the reason for my awakening,
cause for my destruction,
and as mysteriously as he appeared,
He left..
Like the death of a star,
Cosmic event,
I was forced to accept a reality in which

I would no longer learn from his breath,
or grow from his scent.
But I'm grateful, having known him
the time I did.
Having loved him
the chances I could.
Because without him,
my words would not have searched
into prisms of light and color;
of sound and wonder.

Thank you Gera

Same Shit, Different Dollar

New Year's resolutions–
A must do
Will do
Can I even do?
I hate "New Year's"
I hate the need
to start something new,
as if the following year
hadn't been full of
unresolved resolutions and
unfulfilled potential.
As though every effort
you had made
isn't valid in retrospect.

I opted for a vision board this year.
Chose quotes that would inspire me:
"Be authentic and unashamed"
(Because we aren't already so self-absorbed)
"Do what you can, not what you feel you must."
(Because my lazy ass needs more excuses
to not finish)
"Tomorrow is no guarantee, enjoy the sweets
today."
(Because I'm not out of shape as it is)

But the thing about these quotes is that
none of them express
the true fear within me;
That this may as well be
another
stagnant
year.

Still living in the same town.
Still around the same people.
Still eating too much or not enough.
Still making excuses for not striving to be more.
Still no degree.
Still no relationship.
Still…
Still…
Still.

Still nothing to show for,
Except now
I'm 30.
Yay.

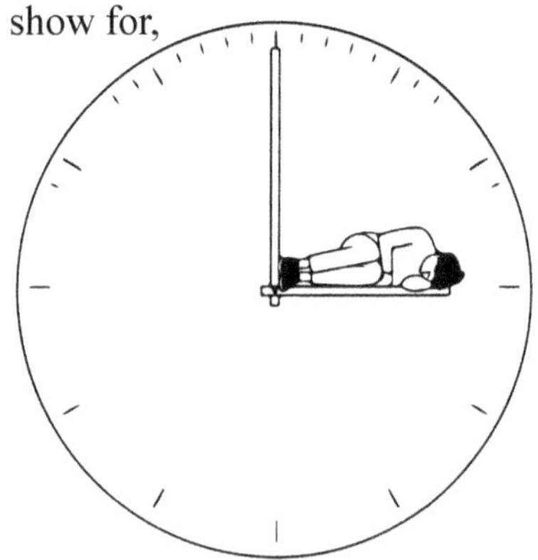

Untitled

The duality of myself
Caged its innocence–
A once-so-hopeful being
stripped away rigorously by
flawed versions of
who I'd come to be,
Yet trying to break free from
the trap that is this body,
Meant for more;
Greatness and splendor
Not here to surrender my
true self
Only self
The art that doesn't sell
The raw, real, and unaccounted for.

Instead my hopes grow silent.
Mind shuts down dreams
even those that seem
quite possible to me.
She laughs in my face and screams
 Failure!

Healing Sunday

My Idea of them versus Reality

I thought he was home,
where my heart could belong.
I thought he was the harmony
to my heart's daily song.

He became a nightmare,
The ones you read about in books.
Dr. Jekyll and Mr. Hyde;
Professional gaslighter
With a narcissistic outlook.
"That's not something I said"
"Let's talk about me instead."
He crushed me
like a bag of old chicken bones,
yet still refuses to leave me alone.

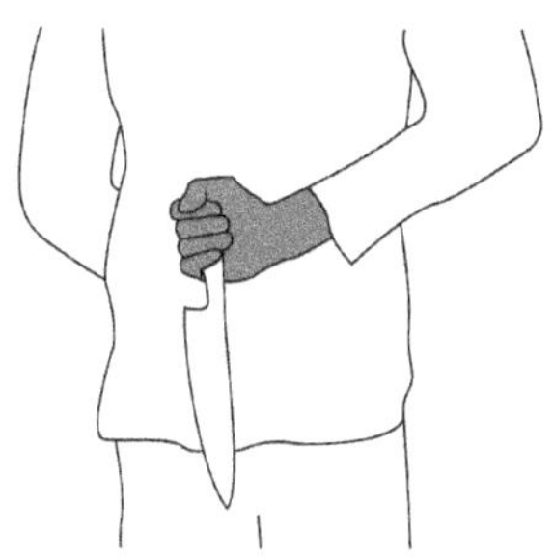

My Heart Must Go On

I love...
So deeply that I get lost in its oceans
Become blinded by emotions
But it's not everyone anymore.
It's not the first glance I get
or the first flirtation I hear.

It's him.
It's been him since 2019,
might be until our kid turns 18
or who knows.
Maybe I'll give up sooner.
Maybe I'll get tired of being that loser
that still clings to a man who
won't give you his world;
who treats your concerns
as if you were a little girl.
Who takes offense when you feel
offended rather than make sure
your heart is defended,
even from himself because
we're not perfect,
we hurt without meaning,
It's part of learning.

To build good beginnings:
listening to each other's needs
and making changes if necessary
to keep each other happy.
And that's what I want,
with him,
and our son.
I want him to be the only one.
But I can't keep holding on to a word
he doesn't give me.
He's miles and miles away,
doesn't even live with me.
I don't see him or smell him,
I don't get to be in his arms.
I don't get to feel safe in them
and away from all harm.

So maybe that's the problem.
Maybe that's what
kills me the most.
It's that I feel like I
am in love with a ghost.

As So Lived Dad

I'm at the point where I want to
bash my head against the wall
until my brains are smeared.
I want to rip my limbs off one
by one
by one.
I want to reach into my chest and
pulverize my heart in my hands
so as to no longer hear its beat.

Anxiety has become my lover
Stress has become my friend
Loneliness my mistress and
Depression my husband.

But you see, I'm a mother.
I'm trying my very best
to raise a human being
that will be good to the rest.
It starts on day one.
The kind of person they will be,
and the last thing I want is
for him to end up like me.
I'm the epitome of broken
battered and beat.

My heart's been abused while
my love's left on the street.
Yet I had the awful habit
of giving it all away.
Now that I'm a mother,
I can't afford the same mistake.
"Guard your heart," I always preached
while I wore it boldly on my sleeve
and expected the rest of the world to
respect that about me.
So touching back on motherhood,
you have to be more firm.
Show them to be tough
in a world that's twisted at each turn.
Yet I have never learned
how to stop from loving
even when it's wrong.
How to stop from singing
when they're tired of your song.
How to not let the gloom
wash away any joy
because the moment you do,
you'll become a toy
to your emotions and your thoughts.
They'll toss you out just anywhere
and you'll be left with the mess
that was a hopeless dreamer's cross to bear.
Each day I wake with a heavy heart.
My soul more dark,

the sky won't part;
there is no silver lining,
No sun among the clouds.
All I see is endless darkness.
All I hear are static sounds.
Until I look over at the face of innocence
and remember what true love is,
remember that sweet bliss.
My frown becoming smile.
My dark becoming day.
But that doesn't mean this joy
is forever going to stay.
Because…
Anxiety has become my lover
Stress has become my friend
Loneliness my mistress and
Depression my husband.

Forgive my Ancestors

How can I explain to those who raised me
That the mold does not fit everyone.

 "I simply can't believe the way you are with
him," she said to me about the way I raise my
child.
 "I never thought this is how you would be."

 "It's called gentle parenting."

 "But YOU are NOT gentle."

It's not a one size fits all.
And why am I not allowed to
break the mold that made me
Not gentle.

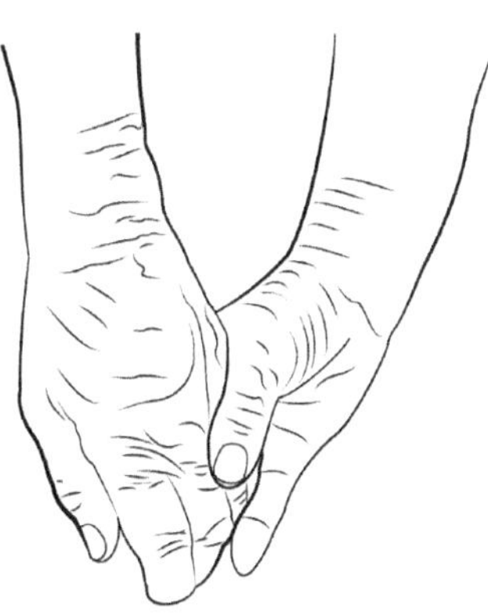

Lifesong

Ate nuts out of a can.
Tried coming up with depressing names
to title my grunge band.
I stopped taking showers
and wore Chanel drenched in depression.
I forgot to water the flowers,
so they were dead by our next session.
The expression
that they had on their face
was the same one I'd get from those
who'd come visit my place. The disgrace
that they felt as they walked in the door
is the same one I saw in the mirror
hours before.
But I swore that I'd feel a lot better,
I'd do more or whatever.
I'd grow and I'd grow and become
self aware. I know
what a cliche, you say.
Like oh come on babe
Just pick up your bags and leave this array
of antique shattered vases like
your heart's little pieces.
All that's missing is a little bull feces
to have them believing that you are ok,
that the world is all rainbow.

Ain't no clouds in your days.
Well I'll paint pretty pictures and
keep switching the masks.
Leave everyone wondering when
the real me will be back.

Love Me or Leave Me

Don't lead me on just because
I check all your boxes.
I am not some pastime
nor a pool to test its waters
or dip your toes in.
I feel deeply,
so when you leave me,
if you leave
High and dry
I don't just cry
I break
and crack
and fall apart
As if you owned my heart
and you probably had
Unwillingly,
Unknowingly,
Unwarranted.

Don't lead me on
because I love hard
. and on instinct.
I know no limits
and dive right in
if my heart wants it.

Don't lead me on
because I'll read into everything;
The stars will write your name.
The flowers will sing your song.
I'll see signs written in dirt,
like the universe itself
has brought us together.

Don't lead me on
because I'll gladly follow
and putting out the fire
is not as easy as lighting its spark.

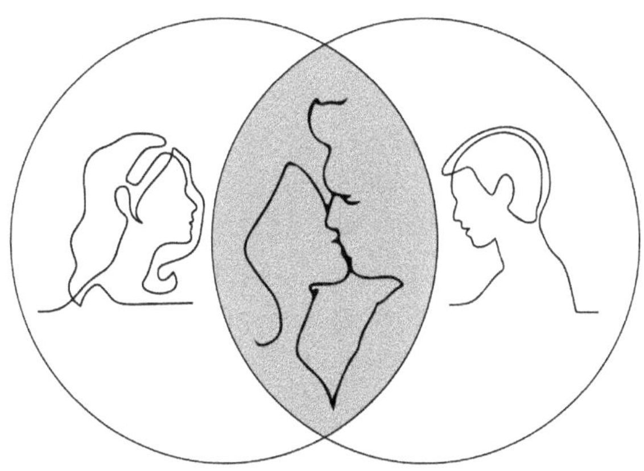

Reality Check

I'm a total disappointment.
I just lay in bed
scrolling through
Instagrams of people instead
of living my own life.
It seems as though I'm stuck inside
the same rut I'd offend
with my "I'm tired of you living
your mediocre life"
But when I had to stand from the fall,
no one even thought twice
about reaching out their hand.
It's probably just due
to the fact that everyone is too
self-consumed to
look back on the ones
that they hurt through
the process of their growth.
Because see right now I'm hurting
and my emotions are all broken
In a way I cannot mend,
I've used duck tape,
I've used glue,
I've even played pretend
but it just wouldn't do.
Falsely smiling at strangers

as though they gave a shit
but I forget each person is focused
on the drama they carry within.
The falsehood of humanity.
We only care until we don't
and by the time that happens
we find caring a simple joke,
By laughing at the broken and
shitting on the pain
as if a little poop would
make it all the same.

But I'm sure that there's a reason,
A cause for this fall;
A purpose to depression.
I'm sure death's taunt isn't all.

I've tried writing you poems,
Tried smoke signals to
get through your head
but the way I see it is
that you're not getting them.
All I want is a sign that
I'm going to be ok.
A sign that all those promises
weren't just words for you to say.
Truth is I didn't ask you
to come save me
or heal my hurt.

All I wanted was an embrace
not some emotional outburst.
But you teased around the pain
I confessed one day
and you kept on acting as though
everything was the same.

I was made for greatness.
I was called to make known
the words in our souls
that we often leave alone.
I was put here to relate
the pain that we all feel,
And due to that
my pain can feel
a thousand times more real.
I feel
too intensely
which makes them not want to stay.
But even with sadness in the way,
I've still managed to get somewhere.
I'm still growing everyday.

Deep Dark Secrets

Depression
is what my therapist said
while I sat in a chair
across from her desk
and shared my life's story
with its infinite messes;
like how he left me alone
raising a child on my own
and I own absolutely
nothing to help me
get ahead of the thoughts
that drown me and fill me with dread.
Depression, that bitch
resides rent-free in my mind.
She's always a downer,
never is kind.
She reminds me of failures.
Tells me I suck,
and not in a good way
but in the way that life fucks
me from behind when
I try to advance
yet I don't give myself a chance
to stand up to her
because she's just so heavy.
Like a fat cat

laying on my chest
leaving no room to breathe.
She's mean
and warm
and somehow comforting,
which is why I find myself
always sleeping
with her, in my bed
instead of love
or a man.
It's because she now owns me
in the palm of her hand

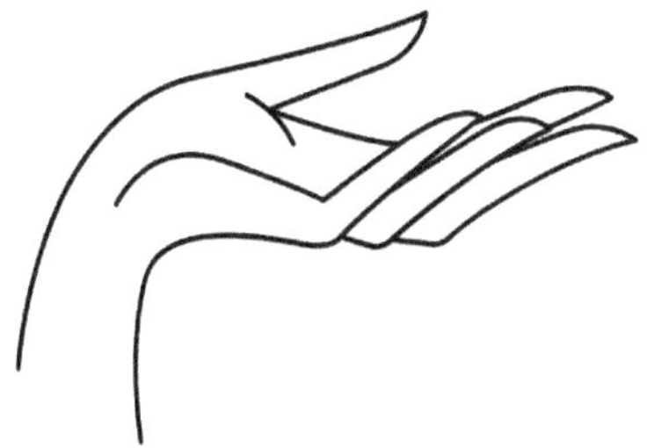

Dear Future Self

Please say no to exes who
ask for second chances.
Please value yourself enough to respect
the boundaries that you have set.
Don't allow just any man the
privilege of knowing your depths.
Don't forget the hardships you've endured
in order to arrive at the place of self-worth
that you currently find yourself in.
Set clear boundaries that shout their truths.
Acknowledge the effort
you've put into healing and
celebrate the growth it has brought.
Don't believe any unwarranted opinions given
by others who have not taken the time
to fully learn and study you.
Be gracious with your mistakes and
Generous with your successes.
Throw yourself parties and
pop the champagne.
Life is too short to waste on regrets;

But please,
Please say no to exes.

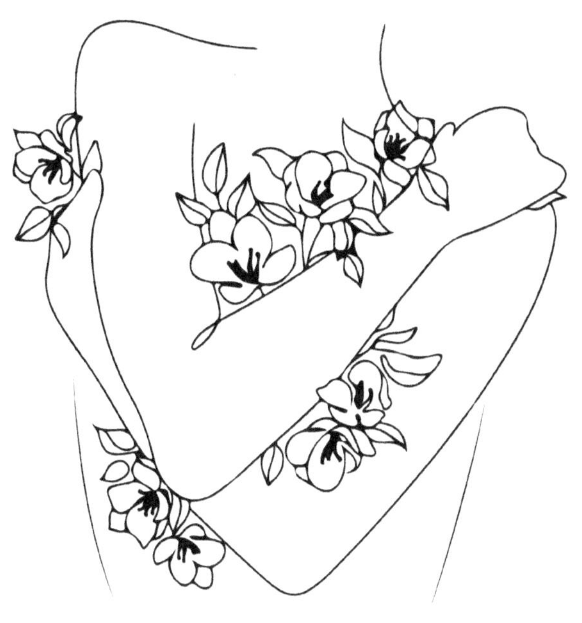

Count Woes

I'm wearing two hats,
They're heaving as fuck
with each passing day
I feel one added on.
I'm wearing three hats
and I wish to take them off,
but the coat rack I had
broke last fall.
And I'm afraid to leave them
lying on the ground
out of fear they'll be stepped on,
leaving me without.

Though if that happens,
How bad would it be?
To rid myself of hats that
seem too heavy for me.

I'm wearing four hats;
Mom
Worker
Student
and me.
The latter being forgotten
by the former three.

Now five hats.
I'm Dad, I forgot to add.

I'm wearing six hats, and
I can't put them down.

Seven Eight Nine
and I ate until 10.
I'd kill for a break
I just don't know when.

Add one more hat.
Eleven is me,
wearing too many hats
at a hundred degrees.

I've begun crying for help,
even when it hurts to ask.
Because I know I need people
to help me carry these hats.

Hear My Prayer

My life's become a clusterfuck.
My house has been a mess.
I'll be waking at all hours
just to get inside my head.

The thing I grew up cringing at
is the thing that I've become.
And I can't quite figure out how to get it
All done.
I'm reaching to an age where
maturity should be primal
yet everything I say and do
and everything I think
seems childish and foolish.
I feel I'm on the brink of
Madness and chaos
even more than in my noggin.
My heart it palpitates.
My thoughts all scramble.
I'm tired,
at a loss
but not yet in shambles.
I'm headed there though
if I keep it up.
Listening to the anxiety,
the creaking on the floor next door.

Heartbeat under floorboards–
My floorboards.
Then whose heartbeat can that be?
Is it that of hopes and dreams?
I'm sure those still live deep inside me.

It must be motivation to go about my day.
The loss of aspiration to grow in every way.
I get lost inside my phone screen
reading comments made by strangers
on another stranger's post or pic.
I might just be in danger
of getting caught inside a cycle;
that thing called going through the motions.
Time slips away while I spend
hours lost in oceans of
space between my fingers
and I don't know how to budge it.
My life is great,
I can't complain,
though complacency has become my partner.
I hope things change
in a good way,
Now that I've come crying to the altar.

1993

It's my birthday today,
All I want to do is sleep.
Depression having a chokehold on me.
Mom wanted to go clubbing
even though I hardly drink.
It's not that I don't like to.
I just prefer being sober, you see.
But buy me birthday shots
if that's something you want for me.
I might get a little tipsy,
not too flirty
though I am 30
so who knows.
The night is young,
we've still got some
time left before last call.
Damn, that's how 30 feels.
Not really but sort of.
Though I now wear confidence like a bra,
Every damn day
even when it weighs
or when it barely stays.
But I wear it.
Like a crown through
all the frowns I get from
people who give me the look of,

"Mmmm you came out in that?"
Why yes. Yes I did
Why the hell not?
I'm still pretty hot
I thought.
But I don't always feel it–
Depression.
Some days get better while others feel worse.
Like a bunch of bricks being
carried in my purse.
And this poem I wrote is truly everywhere,
So forgive me for asking you to not stare.
Or do stare,
if it's what you like,
I can't really blame you
with a face like mine.
Ha! See I told you I wear confidence
Loud and proud.
This was supposed to be a birthday poem:
To talk about the beauty of aging,
To relay feelings of waning
and longing for the girl I lost several hours ago.
But I feel like aged parm,
the good kind of stinky.
Like an excellent wine
that you drink with your pinky,
up in the air
with your long hair flowing
with your whole life ahead

not even knowing
that the clock stops at midnight
even if you're not done.
This poem turned dark,
but that's how it is when death comes.

Up On Cloud 9

I live in love with love.
Romanticize the heartbreak.
Long for a someone
whom to share my life with.
Yet demand so much
that none can keep up.
I wish to be worshiped,
seated above
all other
priorities,
desires or
wants.
You see, I've come a long way
from where I first started.
Back then I hated every flaw
that I flaunted.
Today I admire
every single imperfection.
Trace with my fingertips
the lines of creation.
The stretch marks love left me,
I remind them "you're ok."
The razor bumps and clumps
that make me imperfectly human
in every way.

Stretchy skin,
uneven skin tone—
I no longer bother
to mention them as I stare
in the mirror.
My vision clearer:
I love myself,
and all that I am. So
Why should I settle for less from a man?

Woman

I am
the product of my own creation.
Put myself in situations,
making messes of my innards.
Hypothetically that is
until it's not.
Until I find myself with guts, spilling out
words outwards,
blood on the floor, heart torn
pieces of it scattered around,
like glass shattered on ground,
and it was
my fault because
I let it happen,
because I felt too much,
because they did not feel enough.
So that gave them the right to
take what was mine and
break it until it was not fine,
until I was not fine,
until I had to find
myself again.
And I did.
Through heartache and heartbreak,
Through words of poetry,
Through child's eyes and wonder.

I did.
Not them,
Not he,
No one but me.

So I worship myself
in the dead of night.
I glorify my strength
through the hard fight.
My perseverance and resilience.
Even when I could no more,
I crashed through walls
and tore down doors.
Stepped into my power and
accepted my fate.

I am mother of creation
and between my legs,
the gate.

A list of things to heal your soul

1) a warm bath with scented candles
2) drinking herbal tea
3) basking in the sun
4) hours of laughter with someone you love
5) picking out flowers that make you smile
6) baking cookies
7) sharing a doobie with a homie
 (if that's your thing)
8) dancing in the middle of your living room
9) acknowledging that it's ok to feel things
10) creating something with your hands
11) being grateful

If you feel as though your soul needs healing
and these steps have not helped;
Please seek therapy.

Homebound

At an open mic night
is where I wanted to be.
Spitting words,
Dropping bombs,
Like it was for me,
way back when
I would rush
after 7 hour shifts
to spit lyrics
I would write
like a smoothly laid out diss.
But way back when
I would rush
on my own time and clock.
I would move to my rhythm
as if I could never stop.
Now I rush
to the call
of my proudest creation.
He I birthed;
Formed within
without wrong
or limitation.
Now I rush
to pick him up
after 8 hour shifts

to spend as much time
as I possibly can with him.
And I sit here on the couch
instead of at a late brewery.
Thinking,
"How I love my life!"
I'd choose it again if you asked me.
My life
with my Sun,
My gravitational pull.
Even when all feels too heavy
My heart is still full.

Seeing Yourself

Today I saw myself
for the first time when
I allowed love to take me.
My child running up to me,
saying, "ooh mama so pretty".
The thought of self-doubt
shedding away as he
held me tightly and
engulfed me in his embrace.
How could I not see?
the miracle of my body,
having housed and birthed this
Grandeur of love,
reminding me that
She, too, longs to be
acknowledged for her magic.
She is magic.
I am magic,
And I will no longer forget.

I wept and sighed at how
I never thanked her, my body.
Her beautiful curves
mapping every struggle and hardship
that life has put us through.

I deserve
to accept that I am worthy.
to see myself as my child sees me.
As the world that spins in orbit.
As the cosmos that move the oceans.
I am mother,
Supernova.

Aquatic Sun

Roaring tidal waves crash in as
I slowly dip my toes into the water.
No stranger to adventure, I venture
conquering every rubber duck and plastic cup
in my way.
"Steer clear of the paper shark though," I say.
While my maker,
often times dream breaker,
tells me to sit;
I throw a fit.
Who does she think she is?
This is my ocean and my ship.
And if she's got a problem with it
well I'll just throw her overboard, yes
it seems I'm very bored so I'll cry and I'll
cry until she pulls the ocean's stopper–
drains the water, that'll stop her.
But she says that I'm not done
since we've only just begun.

So I guess I'm off to captain now,
to steer us in the right direction.
All the while,
she'll wash the child
in case I forgot to mention.

This ocean that I'm navigating
is really quite something.
Woah! Here come the bubbles,
and yellow submarines.
I'm trying to imagine life without this storm
except she keeps pouring water,
Hmm, it actually feels warm.
Ok I guess it feels nice to sit here and relax
while this lady I call mother finishes my bath.